MOUNTAINS

A Cherrytree Book

Designed and produced by
A S Publishing

First published 1989
by Cherrytree Press Ltd
a subsidiary of
The Chivers Company Ltd
Windsor Bridge Road
Bath, Avon BA2 3AX

Copyright © Cherrytree Press Ltd 1989

British Library Cataloguing in Publication Data

Mariner, Tom
   Mountains.
   1. Mountains. For children
   I. Title II. Atkinson, Mike III. Series
   551.4'32

   ISBN 0-7451-5046-2

Printed in Italy by Imago Publishing Ltd

EARTH IN ACTION
MOUNTAINS

By Tom Mariner
Illustrated by Mike Atkinson

CHERRYTREE BOOKS

What are Mountains?

A mountain is an area of the Earth's surface which rises considerably above the surrounding land. It often has steep, rocky sides that are difficult to climb. Many mountains form part of much larger areas of high ground. A group or line of mountains is called a mountain range or chain.

Mountains cover more than a quarter of the world's surface. Even under the sea, there are mountain ranges, some of which emerge from the water as islands. The West Indies are an example.

Some mountain ranges include areas of fairly level land, which are almost as high as the mountain tops. These high plains are called *plateaus*.

Mount Everest is the world's highest mountain. It is one of 109 peaks which rise more than 7300 metres high, 96 of which are in the Himalaya and Karakoram ranges in central Asia. Their peaks are snow-covered all the year round because they are so high.

The height of a mountain is always worked out as the height above mean, or average, sea level (even though the sea may be a long way from the mountain). It is never given as the height above the surrounding land. To be called a mountain, the land must generally be more than 700 metres above sea level. High ground lower than that is called a hill.

The greatest mountain range on Earth is the Himalayas. It contains most of the world's highest peaks, including Mount Everest, the highest of all, which stands on the border between Nepal and China. The western parts of North and South America contain huge mountain chains, notably the Rocky Mountains in North America and the Andes in South America.

Some mountains are active volcanoes. They are formed from hardened lava, fine ash and other material which has poured out of the mouth of the volcano. At the top of some active volcanoes, runny lava is hurled into the air, forming fire fountains.

Plates on the Move

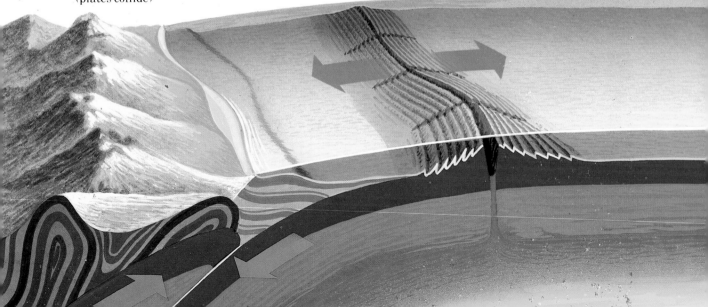

The diameter of the Earth is more than 12,700 kilometres. The oceanic crust is on average only 6 km thick, as compared with the continental crust which, on average, is 35–40 km thick.

The Earth is a sphere formed of layers of rock. At the centre is the *core*, made mostly of iron. Around it is a thick layer of heavy rock called the *mantle*. Near the top of the mantle it is so hot that the rocks have melted. This molten rock, called *magma*, acts like a liquid. The hard, rocky outer layers of the Earth – the crust and the solid top part of the mantle – float upon this molten layer.

The hard outer layer of the Earth is split into several large pieces, called plates. Currents in the molten rock in the upper mantle, between about 70 to 100 kilometres below the surface, cause the plates to move. The movements are slow – only a few centimetres a year. But over millions of years plate movements split continents apart, create new oceans, and crumple rocks into huge mountain ranges.

Fold mountains
(plates collide)

Oceanic ridge
(plates move apart)

When two plates drift apart, magma rises to fill the gap between them. It quickly hardens into rock. As the drifting continues, more and more magma rises to form new crustal rock. This is how the oceans formed.

The Atlantic Ocean began as a split between two plates, about 140 million years ago. A huge mountain range now runs down the middle of this ocean. In the middle of it is a deep valley. It marks the edges of the two plates. Hot magma is rising up along the valley, gradually widening the Atlantic Ocean.

When plates made of continental crust collide, the edges of both plates are buckled up into mountain ranges. When an oceanic plate collides with a plate capped by a continent, the oceanic plate is pushed under the continental plate along a deep trench on the ocean floor. The continental crust is folded into a mountain chain. The Andes Mountains of South America were formed in this way.

When plates move apart, water flows in to fill the space and oceans are formed. When plates collide, they make trenches or mountains. As the crust crumples and folds, weak points widen into cracks. The descending plate is melted and turned into magma. Some of this magma rises through the cracks and reaches the surface through volcanoes. This is happening in the Andes Mountains of South America.

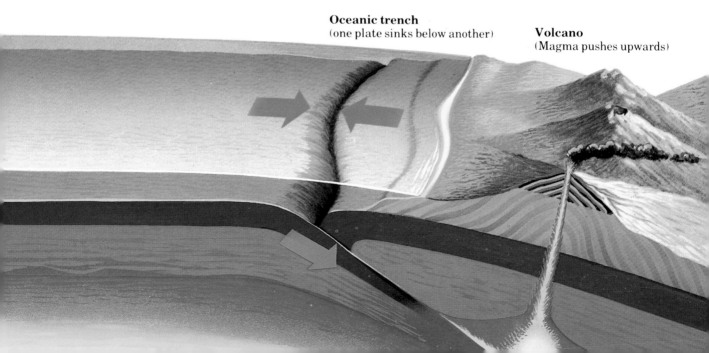

Oceanic trench
(one plate sinks below another)

Volcano
(Magma pushes upwards)

Volcanoes

There are over 500 active volcanoes on dry land, three-quarters of which lie around the Pacific Ocean. Most volcanoes lie near plate edges. Some lie near ocean trenches where descending plates are melted. Others lie on the ocean ridges where plates are moving apart. A few volcanoes lie far from plate edges. The magma from these volcanoes is probably produced by a *hot spot* – an isolated source of heat in the mantle.

The magma contains a high proportion of gas, held under enormous pressure deep in the Earth. When it erupts at the surface the gas escapes and the magma

Opposite: In a typical explosive volcano (1), pressure from the fiery, gas-filled magma builds up until it explodes with massive force, hurling rocks, steam, ash, and large lumps of molten lava into the air. In time, a tall cone builds up around the vent with a crater at the top.

The runny lava that quietly spills out when a shield volcano (2) erupts builds up a flatter mound.

Between eruptions a volcano is said to be dormant (sleeping). Volcanoes where all activity has ceased are extinct (3).

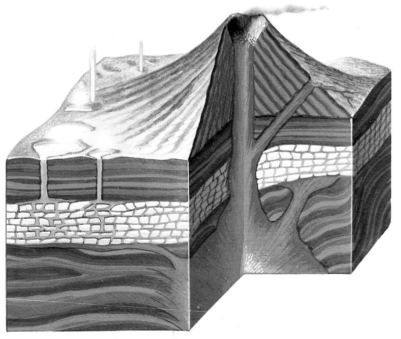

Most volcanoes are intermediate. They may erupt explosively or quietly, and build up slopes of ash and lava. Lava may spill from vents in the sides, and nearby there may be geysers and hot springs with water heated by the magma below ground.

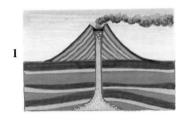

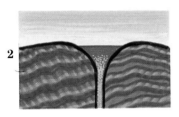

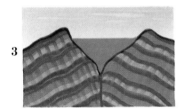

becomes *lava*. If the lava is thin and runny, the gas escapes easily and the eruption is said to be 'quiet'. If the lava is thick, the trapped gas explodes and shatters the lava in pieces, producing an 'explosive' eruption of rock, dust and ashes.

Thin lava spreads over a wide area around the vent, through which it emerges. Successive lava flows build up into a gently sloping dome, like an upturned saucer. Such volcanoes are called *shield volcanoes*. Iceland and the Hawaiian islands have large shield volcanoes.

Thick lava does not flow easily. The dust and rock produced when it explodes pile up round the vent, forming a cone-shaped hill called a *strato-volcano*. Some huge cone-shaped mountains like Mount Fuji in Japan, or Mount Egmont in New Zealand are made of alternate layers of volcanic ash and other fragments from explosive eruptions and lava from quiet ones.

The map shows the plates into which the Earth's crust is divided and marks the major active volcanoes. Notice how many follow the line of the plate boundaries around the Pacific Ocean in a 'Ring of Fire'.

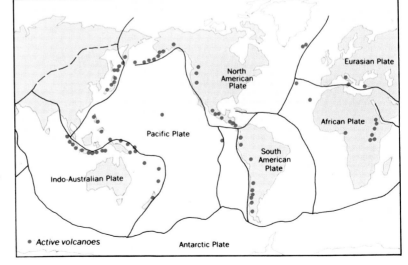

- Active volcanoes

Eurasian Plate
North American Plate
African Plate
Pacific Plate
South American Plate
Indo-Australian Plate
Antarctic Plate

9

When the Land is Folded

Rocks deep in the Earth are hot. They can be melted or bent like slabs of warm toffee. Cold rocks at the surface are hard and brittle. Instead of bending, these rocks tend to break as they fold, crumbling up into mountains as plates collide. Simple folds are synclines and anticlines. An anticlinorum is a collection of anticlines.

There are three kinds of mountains: *volcanoes, fold* mountains and *block* mountains. The world's greatest mountains, the Himalayas, the Rockies, the Andes and the European Alps are all fold mountains. These ranges were all formed as a result of one plate colliding with another, and causing enormous sideways pressure on the rocks.

Originally the rocks were flat. Many were formed from sediments, such as clay and sand, laid down on the sea bed in layers, called *strata*, like the layers in a sandwich. The pressure of the collision caused them to bend and twist, rise up to great heights and tower over

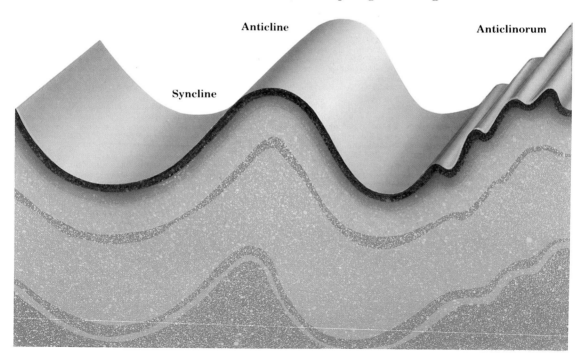

Anticline

Anticlinorum

Syncline

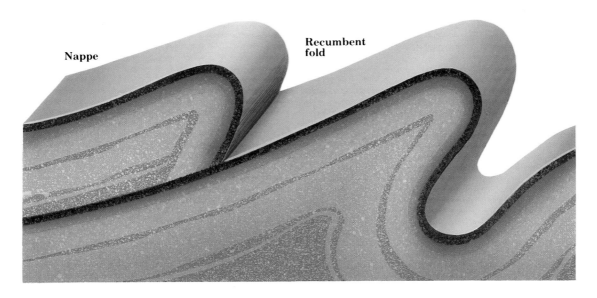

Nappe

Recumbent fold

the older continental masses on either side. Where once there was ocean, now there is land.

The Himalayas were formed when the plate carrying India pushed against the plate carrying the rest of Asia. The rocks on the sea bed were squeezed together and forced upwards. Fossils of sea creatures have been found high in the mountains, and are evidence that the land was once under the sea.

Types of Folds

Folds occur in many shapes and sizes: some are mere crinkles, a few metres long, others may be huge. A downward fold, like a trough, is called a *syncline*; an upward fold, like an arch, is called an *anticline*. A fold lying on its side is called a *recumbent* fold. Sometimes, a recumbent fold is snapped. The upper half is pushed sideways some distance over the lower half. A fold broken like this is called a *nappe*.

Some folds turn on their sides. These are called recumbent folds. Sometimes folds are snapped and are pushed up over other rocks. These are called nappes.

You often cannot see the original shape of a fold mountain, because the surface rocks have been worn away by erosion.

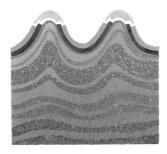

Land at Fault

When two plates meet head on, or scrape against each other, the rocks between them either bend into folds, or they break. Breaks or fractures in rock strata are called *faults*.

Faults usually occur in groups and some extend for thousands of metres down into the Earth's crust. If two deep faults occur roughly parallel to each other, the block of land between may be heaved up to form a block mountain, or dropped to make a steep-sided *rift valley*. The Ruwenzori Mountains on the equator in Central Africa are 80 kilometres across and over 5000 metres high. They are an example of a huge block of crust uplifted between faults.

Some block mountains have flat tops and form high plateaus. Others, such as the Black Forest and the Vosges Mountains in Europe, form long ridges.

When rock strata break, the broken ends are forced up or down along the crack. This is called a fault.

Block mountains and rift valleys form between parallel sets of faults. Sudden movements of rocks, unable to stand the enormous strain and pressure put on them, cause earthquakes.

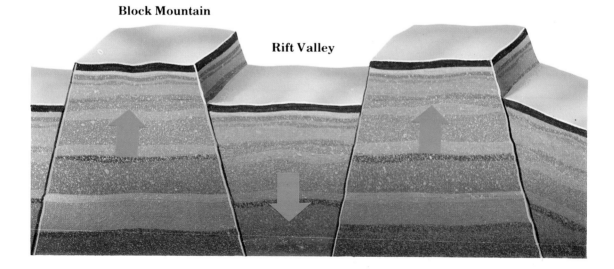

Block Mountain

Rift Valley

Dome Mountains

Only a little of the magma which rises from the mantle into the Earth's crust ever reaches the surface. Most of it forces its way between layers of rock in the crust and becomes trapped there. Eventually it cools and sets into hard rock, such as granite. Rocks formed in this way are called *intrusive* rocks.

Intrusive rocks may be thin sheets, or huge masses many kilometres wide and deep. When huge bodies of magma rise through the crust, they may push the overlying rock layers into a huge dome mountain.

Rocks formed when the magma cools and hardens under the ground are usually tougher and harder than the rocks above and around them. We can see granite rocks formed from molten magma in many places where the overlying, softer rocks have been worn away by frost, ice and running water. For example, the Cairngorm Mountains in Scotland and the Sierra Nevada range in California are made of intrusive rocks that have been exposed on the surface.

EARTHQUAKES
An earthquake is caused when a piece of the Earth's crust breaks, or when two plates rub against each other. The sudden movement starts shock waves, which travel outwards like ripples on a pond, causing the Earth's surface to heave and shake.

When magma rises through the Earth's crust, it forces up the overlying rock layers into a dome mountain. In time the surface layers may wear away, leaving bare igneous rock.

'Rocky' Mountains

There are three kinds of rock in the Earth's crust: *igneous*, *sedimentary* and *metamorphic*.

Igneous Rocks

The word igneous comes from the Latin word for fire. Igneous rocks are formed when hot magma in the crust, or lava on the surface, cools and hardens. Igneous rock can be *intrusive* (meaning forced in) or *extrusive* (meaning forced out).

Granite is the commonest type of intrusive rock. It forms when magma forced up into the Earth's crust

Basalt
(extrusive igneous)

Obsidian
(extrusive igneous)

Granite
(intrusive igneous)

Marble
(metamorphic)

14

Conglomerate
(sedimentary)

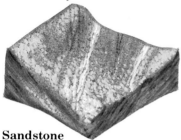

Sandstone
(sedimentary)

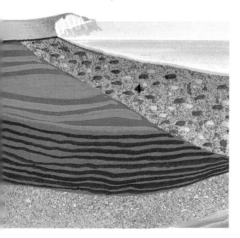

Intrusive igneous rock(1)
and metamorphic rock (2)
are formed below ground.

Extrusive igneous rock(3)
is formed above ground.
Most sedimentary rocks
(4) form under the sea.

cools down underground, without reaching the surface. Magma forced to the surface through volcanoes or faults becomes lava and cools to form extrusive rocks, such as basalt and obsidian.

Sedimentary Rocks

Rocks all over the Earth are constantly worn down and broken into particles of sand, soil and mud. These sediments are washed by the rain into rivers and are carried away to the sea. Once in the sea, they settle on the sea floor. Layers of sand, mud, pebbles and the shells of sea creatures pile up and eventually harden into sedimentary rock. The word sediment comes from the Latin word meaning to settle or sink down.

Sedimentary rocks include sandstone, limestone and puddingstone. Sandstone consists of layers of sand pressed together and cemented by chemicals which seep from the water. Limestone is mostly made from tiny dead sea creatures, whose remains piled up in their billions on the sea bed and built up into enormous thicknesses of rock. Puddingstone is a *conglomerate* rock consisting of a 'pudding' of pebbles, sand and mud.

Metamorphic Rocks

Great heat and pressure in the crust can change rocks into new forms. The heat comes from molten areas nearby, the pressure from the weight of overlying rock or earth movements. Rocks that are changed in this way are called metamorphic rocks, after two Greek words meaning change and form. Marble is a metamorphic rock, formed when limestone in the Earth's crust is subjected to great heat and pressure.

Wearing Mountains Down

Mountains begin to be worn down, or *eroded*, as soon as they are formed. The main tools of erosion are running water, heat, frost, ice and, in dry areas, wind. Most erosion takes place slowly, but occasionally landslides and rock falls achieve as much in a few minutes as the other kinds of erosion achieve in a thousand years.

Rivers begin high in the mountains. The rushing water carves out a valley by eroding the mountainside. Heavy rain splashes grains of soil into the air and washes them down steep mountainsides into the river. Even on the gentle slopes, soil is on the move. Every time rain falls, it eases the soil a little more downhill, in a movement called soil creep. The movement may be only 10 centimetres in a hundred years, but it occurs over the whole surface of the slope. In time the hillside will creep to the bottom of the valley.

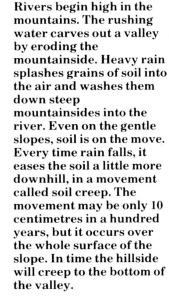

The slow wearing down of rocks is called *weathering*. In hot places, rocks may be heated during the day and get very cold at night. Repeated changes in temperature weaken the surface of the rocks and pieces fall off.

In cool, rainy places, water seeps into cracks in rocks and freezes into ice. When water turns to ice, it increases in size by about a tenth. As it freezes, the ice pushes against the sides of the cracks and forces them further apart. After this has happened many times, the rocks may shatter or be split in two.

Pieces of rock that have broken off slide down the mountainside. Gradually they pile up into sloping banks of stones and boulders called *scree*.

As rain falls, it dissolves a gas in the air and becomes acidic. The acid is weak, but strong enough to eat away limestone rock. Mountains made of limestone are worn down in this way.

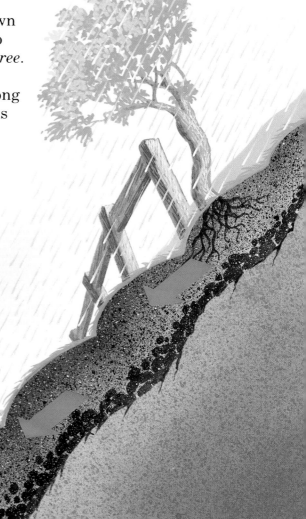

Heavy rain on steep slopes sometimes causes landslides. The soil becomes saturated and some of it 'floats' on the rainwater. On a steep slope, there may be nothing to hold the soil back and large slabs of it slither downwards, smashing everything in their path. Trees growing naturally, or planted, on hillsides help to prevent floods and avalanches. Their roots bind the soil and help it soak up water. Their foliage acts as an umbrella over the soil.

Ice in Action

High up in the mountains the air is cold. Most of the moisture which falls there is snow. Below a certain level, the snow melts in summer, but in higher parts it remains all year round. The lower limit of this perpetual snow is called the *snow line*.

Above the snow line, the snow piles up, year after year. The fresh snow weighs down on the snow beneath it and after years of pressure the bottom snow becomes ice. As it gets thicker, the ice grows heavier and gradually moves downhill under its own weight. The snow has become a glacier, a river of ice.

Like rivers, glaciers flow down valleys. A glacier gouges out a valley with a U-shape. Rocks embedded in the ice scrape away at the valley bottom.

Glaciers are very powerful. As they move down a mountainside they pluck up rocks which grind away the rock beneath. They move partly because of gravity and partly because of melting. For example, when a thin layer of ice on the bottom and sides of glaciers melts, the ice above it slides forward. When the water refreezes, rocks become embedded in it. They are carried away, scraping away at the land as they move along. At the end of the glacier, the rocks carried on top of and inside the glacier are dumped as moraine.

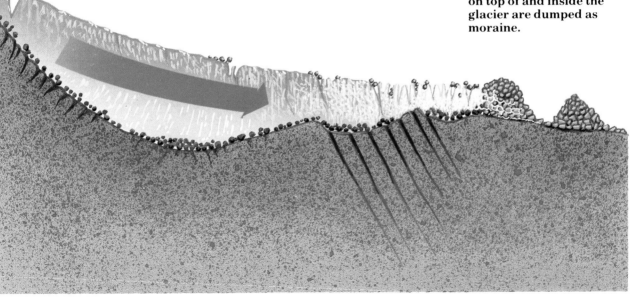

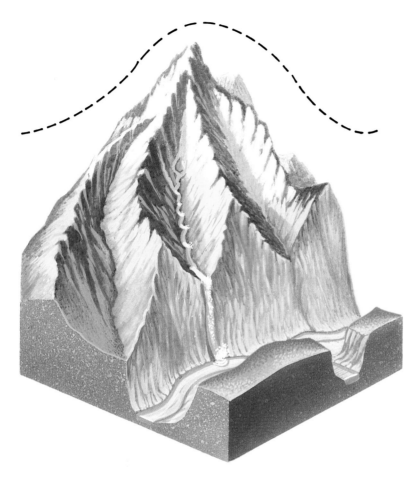

Once this mountain was the shape of the dotted line. Snow piled up on its surface and turned to ice. The ice carved out steep basins called cirques on the sides of the mountains. These grew bigger and eventually reduced the mountain to a jagged peak, shaped like a pyramid. The ridges between cirques are called arêtes. Streams from the melting ice became rivers.

Many features of mountain scenery result from the work of ice. The basins, or *cirques*, where a glacier once formed are steep-sided. Knife-edged ridges, called *arêtes*, separate neighbouring cirques. Broad-bottomed, steep-sided valleys are gouged out by ice. Tall waterfalls pour down from their sides, while lakes lie in hollows scraped out by ice. Mounds of frost-shattered clay and rock, called *moraine*, lie discarded by the melting ice at the end of the glacier.

Mountains and Climate

When moving air meets a mountain, it is forced to rise. Rising air cools. As it cools, the invisible moisture it contains condenses to form rain or snow, which falls to the ground below. When the air has passed over the crest of the mountains it sinks to lower levels on the other side. As the air sinks it gets warmer and dries the land it passes over. Thus, the air which has dropped its moisture on one side of the mountain becomes warm and dry as it descends the other side.

The Rocky Mountains in North America stand in the way of moist winds blowing off the Pacific. The slopes facing the ocean have high rainfall, while the land on the other side gets little rain and is desert in some areas.

When warm winds blow across the sea, they pick up water – in the form of invisible vapour. When the winds hit the land, the air rises and cools. Clouds form as the water vapour condenses, and rain falls. As it flows down the other side of the mountain – the leeside – the air becomes warmer, so the weather there is hot and dry. The far side of a mountain is said to be in a rain shadow.

Mount Kilimanjaro
5895m – 5°S

Mount McKinley
6194m – 62°N

Matterhorn
4477m – 45°N

As you climb a mountain, the air gets colder. The temperature falls by about 2°C for every 300 metres of height. The reason for this is that the air is thinner and the particles of dust and moisture in the air, which trap and give out heat received from the Sun, get fewer with height. Thus the clearer mountain air captures less warmth from the Sun's rays than the dustier, moist air lower down.

It is very cold in the mountains after dark. The clear air loses heat quickly at night. The rocks may be heated to a blistering temperature by the direct rays of the Sun during the day, but at night most of this heat escapes rapidly back into space.

Mountain climates are harsh. Winters are longer and more severe, spring comes later, and summers are cooler and shorter than in the valleys and lowlands.

The snow line is the level on a mountain above which snow lies all year long. Its height varies with the distance of the mountain from the equator. Near the poles, the snow line is at sea level. At the equator it rises above 5000 metres. Mount McKinley in Alaska is almost completely snow-clad all the year round, whereas only the peak of Africa's Mount Kilimanjaro is, despite its height.

21

Plants of the Mountains

As the temperature gets colder going up a mountain, so the kinds of plants that live there change. Tropical forest often grows at the foot of mountains on the equator. About a thousand metres higher, the climate becomes too cold for tropical vegetation. Trees and plants similar to those in cooler regions take its place. Higher up the mountain, these give way to coniferous trees, hardy enough to withstand long periods of cold weather. Higher still, even these cannot survive. This level, where the trees end, is called the *tree line*.

Mountain Flowers

Above the tree line, and below the edge of permanent snow towards the summit, is a stretch of mountainside inhabited by special kinds of plants called *alpines*. They do not grow naturally anywhere else. They have developed special foliage, flowers, shapes and ways of growing that make them able to survive in the harsh mountain conditions.

Alpines are short, squat plants. They lie low to avoid damage from the bitter winds which blow constantly at high levels. They have long, slender roots which travel deep into the rocks in search of every scrap of food and water. The growing season is short and their flowers form quickly. Their petals are dark to absorb heat and especially vivid, so that insects will be attracted to them and pollinate them before their brief flowering period is over.

On high mountain slopes, the thin soil is frozen for months on end, so alpines must survive for long periods without moisture.

MOUNTAIN PLANTS
Just as vegetation varies as you go from the equator to the poles, so the vegetation on a mountain changes. At the top, no plants can survive in the bitter winds and perpetual snow and ice.

ALPINE MEADOWS
High up, mosses and lichens gain a foothold on the bare rocks. Further down alpine flowers grow, and there are grassy meadows dotted with stunted shrubs.

CONIFEROUS FORESTS
Evergreen trees, with narrow needle-like leaves that lose little moisture and are frost resistant, can stand up to the cold, windy conditions.

TEMPERATE FOREST
Deciduous trees grow lower down where conditions are less harsh. They drop their leaves before winter and become dormant, before springing into new life in the spring. (At the equator, the climate is wet and warm enough for tropical forest to grow 1000 metres up on the mountainside.)

VALLEYS
In the valleys, it is warm and the soil is fertile enough to grow crops and grass.

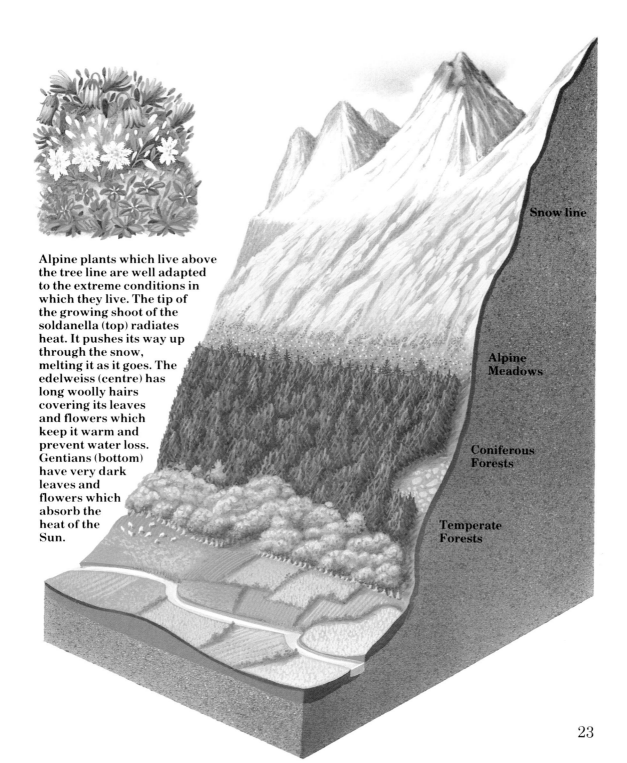

Alpine plants which live above the tree line are well adapted to the extreme conditions in which they live. The tip of the growing shoot of the soldanella (top) radiates heat. It pushes its way up through the snow, melting it as it goes. The edelweiss (centre) has long woolly hairs covering its leaves and flowers which keep it warm and prevent water loss. Gentians (bottom) have very dark leaves and flowers which absorb the heat of the Sun.

Snow line

Alpine Meadows

Coniferous Forests

Temperate Forests

23

The Rocky Mountain goat (above) has layers of fat under its hide and grows a dense hairy coat. Its short sturdy legs and gripping hoofs enable it to climb almost sheer rock faces in search of food – well out of reach of the mountain lion (below), which preys on the smaller animals lower down the slopes.

Mountain Animals

Mountains above the tree line are bleak, hostile places. Animals that make their homes there have bodies and ways of life which enable them to survive some of the worst conditions on Earth.

Plant-eaters

Most animals that live at high altitudes are plant-eaters. They include many varieties of sheep, goats, deer, yaks, llamas, guanacos and vicuñas. They grow thick coats to keep out the cold. They can climb almost vertically, gripping tiny rock ledges with pincer-like hoofs. They breathe easily in the thin air because of extra-large hearts and lungs. They have blood which absorbs oxygen nearly three times as efficiently as that of human beings.

Small mammals that live in the mountains not only grow long winter coats, but have a high rate of metabolism (conversion of food to energy). The tiny Alpine shrew eats almost continuously and consumes

more than its own weight in food every day. The marmot eats voraciously all summer until it is very fat. When winter comes, it hibernates. Its heartbeat slows, its body temperature falls, and it stays in that state until the following summer. The pica, a distant cousin of the rabbit, stays awake all winter but keeps a store of sun-dried leaves for winter feed.

A golden eagle spots a marmot and swoops down to seize it in its talons. Small scampering animals are forever at the mercy of eagles which can pinpoint their movements from high in the sky.

Meat-eaters

The Asian snow leopard and the American puma, or mountain lion, shelter in dens at night. They emerge by day to hunt over large areas for sheep, goats and smaller prey. Also ready to pick up the smaller creatures are the great eagles which soar over the mountains. They are light in weight for their size and their bodies can work efficiently at great heights. They have exceptionally keen eyesight which enables them to spot their prey at vast distances.

Mountains and People

Life is hard for people who live on high mountains. The climate is harsh and the ground is steep and rugged. But like plants and animals, human beings have become adapted to the conditions at great altitude.

Lowlanders feel sick, get easily tired and are short of breath above 3000 metres, but mountain people are unaffected. Their hearts and lungs are larger than normal, to make up for the lack of oxygen. They are less liable to frostbite because their blood warms the surface of their bodies more efficiently.

It takes more energy to move about on mountains because of the steep slopes. It is harder both to drag loads uphill and to brake their descent. The soil itself has to be kept from slipping. In China and elsewhere entire mountainsides are ridged with terraces built to hold back precious soil. In Nepal, much of the country's food is grown on these narrow ledges.

People who live in the mountains share certain typical characteristics. Because there is little oxygen in the thin air, they develop extra-large lungs and barrel-shaped chests to accommodate them. They are shorter and stockier than lowlanders, their cheeks are padded with fat against the cold, and they have narrow eye slits with a fold of skin over them to keep their eyes from freezing.

Life in the mountains is difficult. Roads have to be built with hairpin bends, farmland has to be terraced and cattle have to be brought down to the valleys in winter.

In mountains at lower levels, these handicaps become advantages. Switzerland is a mountainous country, yet it is very rich. Mountains are part of its wealth. Millions of tourists visit it every year.

People go to mountains for sport and relaxation. Some go to climb mountains, or ski down them. Rugged country, where travel is difficult, is valued for its beautiful scenery.

Farmers on mountains in Norway and Switzerland and in the Andes of South America have adopted similar ways of coping with their mountain climates. Cattle are kept under cover in winter, near the farmhouses in the valley. Once the snow has melted on the upper slopes, the farmers drive the cattle up the mountains to spend the summer on rich pastures high above the farm. This way of farming is called *transhumance*. Milk from the cows is mostly used to make cheese. Swiss cheeses are among the best in the world.

The mountains provide us with two important resources, neither of which is harnessed without problems. Dams, created to generate hydroelectric power from the swift mountain streams, often cause unwelcome environmental changes. The great forests which grow on the mountain slopes have been largely cut down for timber. But the disappearance of the trees has been the cause of terrible floods further down the mountains. Even skiers, enjoying the bracing mountain air and healthy activity, do damage to the mountains, littering the slopes and causing avalanches.

Mountains in Danger

Millions of trees on mountains are dying. Their killer is rain, turned to acid by fumes from factories, homes and traffic in lowlands far away. Millions more are felled for timber or to make way for farmland.

Trees absorb rain, helping it sink into the soil and run gently into rivers. They hold back drifting snow, and anchor soil to steep slopes. Mountains without trees are dangerous. In the Alps, where 50 million visitors a year add to the pollution and destruction, landslides and avalanches are getting more frequent. Almost the whole of Bangladesh was flooded in 1988, by rivers from the Himalayan Mountains. These rivers were swollen by water rushing down from bare slopes where the trees had been removed.

Such disasters will happen more often and in more places, until we learn to look after our mountains.

As well as deliberate felling of trees, which in time can be rectified by replanting, a new hazard faces the mountains – pollution. Industrial air pollution creates 'acid rain' which is carried away from the cities by the winds and dumped on the mountains. Unless pollution controls are tightened, millions of hectares of natural forest will disappear. And if people do not learn to respect the outstanding beauty of mountain areas, they will be used more and more as dumping grounds for unwanted rubbish.

Mountain Profiles

Names in *italics* indicate separate entries.

Aconcagua Peak in Andes (Argentina), highest in South America (6960 m).

Adirondacks Range in northeastern United States. Averages 1200 m in height, with Mt Marcy highest (1630 m).

Alaska Range in southern Alaska which includes *Mt McKinley*, the highest peak in North America.

Alps Range in Western Europe, up to 300 km wide and about 1200 km long. They run from northern Yugoslavia to France, through Italy, Austria, Liechtenstein, Switzerland and West Germany. The Alps are fold mountains, uplifted during the past 25 million years as the African plate has pressed into the European plate. *Mont Blanc* is the highest peak.

Andes Range which stretches for over 6400 km down the western side of South America. In Bolivia and Peru, the Andes broaden into a plateau 600 km wide and 4000 m high. Formed by the collision of two plates, the Andes are mostly fold mountains. The plates are still moving and the Andes are still rising. Many peaks are over 6000 km, including the highest, *Aconcagua.*

Annapurna in the Himalayas in Nepal is the eleventh highest peak in the world (8078 m).

Appalachian Group of mountain ranges in the United States which include the White and the Green Mountains, the Catskills and the Great Smokies. They run for about 2500 km from the state of Maine in the north to Alabama in the south. Old fold mountains, they were uplifted between 250 and 500 million years ago. Once taller than the Himalayas, they have been worn down by millions of years of erosion. The highest peak is *Mt Mitchell.*

Ararat Volcanic mountain in Turkey. Supposed resting place of Noah's ark (5165 m).

Atlas Range in north-western Africa. Ridges of fold mountains which run east-west for 2400 km through Morocco, Algeria and Tunisia. Average height between 2500 and 3000 m. Highest peak is Jebel Toubkal in Morocco (4165 m).

Ben Nevis Extinct volcanic peak in Scotland. Highest in British Isles (1344 m).

Brazilian Highlands An upland region in east-central Brazil, mostly between 300 and 900 m above sea level. It forms a watershed between rivers flowing into the Amazon basin and other rivers flowing east and south into the Atlantic Ocean.

Carpathian Range running for about 1300 km from Czechoslovakia through the Ukraine in the USSR, to Romania. They are fold mountains uplifted at the same time as the Alps. The highest peak, Gerlachovsky Stit, is in Czechoslovakia (2655 m).

Cascade Range in United States stretching from northern California, through western Oregon and Washington, into southern British Columbia. Two volcanoes have erupted this century: Lassen Peak in 1921 and Mt St Helens in 1980. Highest peak is *Mt Rainier.*

Caucasus Range in USSR, stretching for about 1100 km from the Black Sea to the Caspian Sea. *Mt Elbruz* is highest peak.

Cayambe Extinct volcano with square crater in Andes in Ecuador (5958 m).

Chimborazo Extinct volcano in Andes in Ecuador (6286 m).

Citlaltepétl (or Orizaba) Active volcano and highest peak in Mexico (5700 m).

Communism Peak in Pamir range in Tadzik. Highest in the USSR (7495 m).

Cook Mountain in Southern Alps on South Island. Highest in New Zealand (3764 m).

Cotopaxi Volcano in Andes in Ecuador. Long thought to be world's highest active volcano (5898 m). The highest active volcano is now thought to be Ojos del Salado (6885 m) on the Chile-Argentina border.

Drakensberg Range in southern Africa. With Maloti Mountains, stretches through Lesotho and South Africa. Highest peaks are Thabana Ntlenyana (3482 m) and Mont aux Sources (3299 m).

Elbert Highest peak of Rocky Mountains in Colorado in the

United States (4399 m).

Ellsworth Highlands in Antarctica. Peaks stick up through ice sheet. Highest is *Vinson Massif*.

Elbruz Highest peak in Caucasus in USSR, and in Europe (5633 m).

Erebus Antarctica's only active volcano, on Ross Island (3794 m).

Ethiopian Highlands Africa's most extensive mountain and high plateau region, rising to Ras Dashen (4620 m).

Etna Active volcano on Italian island of Sicily. Largest in Europe (3340 m).

Everest Mountain in Himalayas on Tibet-Nepal border. World's highest (8848 m).

Fuji Dormant volcanic mountain on Honshu Island in Japan. Considered sacred by many Japanese (3776 m).

Godwin Austen Mountain in Karakoram range of Himalayas in northern Kashmir. Also called K2. Second highest peak in world (8611 m).

Great Dividing Range System running north-south down eastern side of Australia, with various local names. The Snowy Mountains in the Australian Alps in New South Wales are highest area and include *Mt Kosciusko*.

Himalayas Massive mountain system in central Asia, running from northern Pakistan, through northern India, Bhutan and Nepal, to China. Range forms part of the largest and highest area of mountains on Earth and includes *Mt Everest*, the world's highest peak. Nearby ranges include the Hindu

Kush, the Karakoram, the Siwalik, the Pamirs, the Chang Tang and the *Tien Shan*. Tibet is a vast high plateau in the heart of the area. Glaciers are the source of many great rivers, including the Indus, the Brahmaputra, the Ganges, the Chang Jiang, the Si Kiang and the Huang He. The system began to uplift about 50 million years ago when the plate carrying India collided with the Asian plate. Enormously thick beds of rock which had been laid down between the two continents were folded, crumpled and lifted when they met. Parts of the area are still rising.

Jungfrau Peak in Swiss Alps. Its name means The Madonna (4161 m).

K2 See Godwin Austen.

Kanchenjunga Peak in Himalayas on Nepal-Sikkim border. Third highest in world (8585 m).

Kenya Isolated extinct volcano, about 12 km south of the equator in Kenya in Africa (5199 m).

Kilimanjaro Isolated extinct volcano in Tanzania. Highest peak in Africa (5895 m).

Klyuchevskaya Highest of 18 active volcanoes in Siberia in the USSR. Part of the 'Pacific Ring of Fire' (4748 m).

Kosciusko Peak in Australian Alps in New South Wales. Highest in Australia (2228 m).

Lassen Peak See Cascade.

Logan Peak in Yukon in Canada. Highest peak in Canada and second highest in North America (5951 m).

Mackenzie Range in north east-

ern Canada. Part of Rocky Mountain chain.

Matterhorn Peak in Swiss Alps (4477 m).

Mauna Kea Dormant volcano on island of Hawaii (4205 m).

Mauna Loa Large active volcano on Hawaii (4169 m).

McKinley Peak in Alaska range in United States. Highest in North America (6194 m).

Mitchell Highest peak in Appalachians in North Carolina (2037 m).

Mont Blanc Peak in France. Highest in European Alps (4807 m).

Narodnaya Highest peak in Ural Mountains in USSR, at northern end of the range near the Arctic Circle (1894 m).

Ngauruhoe Active volcano on North Island of New Zealand (2290 m).

Orizaba See Citlaltepétl

Pyrenees Range, some 430 km long, which divides France and Spain. They have been formed during the last 25 million years as Spain has been pushed against France by movements in the Earth's crust. Highest point is the Pic d'Aneto (3404 m).

Rainier Highest peak of Cascade mountains in Washington State in United States (4392 m).

Rocky Mountains System stretching for about 5000 km from Alaska in the north, down the western side of Canada and the United States. The Rockies consist of parallel ranges of high mountains with plateaus between them. In places the Rockies stretch 1500 km inland from the Pacific. They are most-

Mountain Ranges

ly fold mountains which began to be uplifted about 70 million years ago. The highest peak in the Rockies is *Mt Elbert*.

Ruapehu Active volcano on North Island of New Zealand (2797 m).

Ruwenzori Range of block mountains on the Uganda-Zaire border in Africa. The equator runs through the mountains and the snow line is at about 4500 m. Highest peak is Mt Margherita (5109 m).

Snowdon Peak in Wales. Second highest in British Isles (1086 m).

Southern Alps Range of mountains running down western side of South Island, New Zealand. Mountains still being formed and subject to frequent minor earthquakes. Highest point is *Mt Cook*.

Stromboli Active volcanic island near Sicily in Italy (926 m).

Tien Shan Range in central Asia. The highest peak, on the China-USSR border, is Pik Pobedy (Tomur Feng in China), at 7439 m.

Tongariro Active volcano on North Island of New Zealand (1965 m).

Urals Chain in USSR which form part of boundary between Europe and Asia. They run north-south for 2400 km between the Arctic Ocean and the Aral Sea. Like the Appalachians in North America, they were uplifted between 250 and 500 million years ago. Now of moderate height, they may once have been higher than the Himalayas. Highest peak is *Mt Narodnaya*.

Vesuvius Active volcano near Naples in Italy. Numerous eruptions recorded. The most famous, in AD 79, destroyed Pompeii (1277 m).

Vinson Massif Highest peak in Antarctica in Sentinel Mountains in Ellsworth Highlands (5140 m).

Whitney Highest peak in Sierra Nevada range in California. The highest peak in the United States outside Alaska (4418 m).

Zagros Range stretching from eastern Turkey through western Iran. It reaches 4548 m west of the city of Esfahan.

Index